# BLACK AMERICA

# ASKING OURSELVES
# THE TOUGH QUESTIONS

## BOOK ONE

## 2010

## By Sonja Cassandra Perdue

# <u>DEDICATION</u>

**To my people with much love.**

# GENERATIONS

### By Sonja Cassandra Perdue

It is the generation before this generation of madness, that is mad.

A legacy of insanity gifted to the children of the insane.

No passing of discipline or traditions, but writs of guilt, pain and plagues.

A torch of sadness—passes.

It is the generation of sunshine that has left us sightless.

As the children of the blind lead us toward the millennium of darkness.

The generation of choice has left us no choices.

As our world turns and we devour ourselves.

We stare into the eyes of our children, a brilliant reflection of our image.

And, we blame them for what we see.

## _In this moment…_

## _You will become part of a movement._

You will not think as you have been taught.

You will not believe or accept what has been said.

> You will think for yourself and you will define what will be said.

In this time, our time, as it may have been in the very beginning, there was a question, a void, a need, then there was an action, a reaction…an answer.

**? ? ? ? ?**

It was the morning of June 8, 2009, and although "the sun was shining and there was plenty of light," the darkness around me was so thick that I could almost touch it. I could not move.

I could not proceed without asking myself some tough questions. So I sat down at the dining room table with a yellow legal pad and penned "Asking Ourselves the Tough Questions — 2010." And what began as a fleeting moment of inner reflection has evolved into a dialogue with Black America.

The questions are in the order that they flowed forth from me to you. I never changed the order, but eliminated some and added other questions. The last question was not my last thought, but how I chose to end the 2010 session.

These were not letters flowing into words or words into sentences. You are not turning the pages of a book. You are moving through space and time to a different place in the history of the African in America.

All that has been lost will forever be lost. Whether by force or by cooperation, we have given all that will be given. No more. This is our time.

## ? ? ? ? ?

Don't turn this page if you are afraid to journey down a path that may invoke memories and emotions that might just make you uncomfortable. You are about to enter a place within that has long awaited your arrival. This place knows you better than anyone else and now speaks to you.

## This is not a test.

Don't answer the questions as though someone is looking over your shoulder and judging every stroke of your pen. Because it is you who will now be the judge of your own Black consciousness.

If you wish, use a separate sheet of paper to record your answers to these questions. If you wish to share your responses — do so.

"Asking Ourselves The Tough Questions — 2010" is for personal conversations, family dinners, bus rides to work, class study, mornings in the neighborhood coffee shops, and those private moments.

Don't skip questions. You know the correct answer to every question. Who knows you better than you?

As you answer, discuss, and even debate "Asking Ourselves The Tough Questions — 2010," you will feel yourself glowing and growing as each page in this process moves you from here to where you've never been before and drops you right off where you want to be.

This book is not for the academics—we listened to their lectures and read their theses. Nor is it being presented for the opinions of the political actors or media performers with their corporate-sponsored and controlled sound bytes of nothingness.

This book is for you. Sit back and relax with your favorite person and come through this experience with a clearer portrait of *"thyself."*

**Who is Black America?**

**The answer is … <u>You are Black America</u>**

**Sonja Cassandra Perdue**

?

?

?

?

?

2010

# *1*

Imagine that you are a Black man and the year is 1955.  You're walking down the street in the community known as Bridgeport in Chicago and four white men pull up beside you in a Chevy.

Are you afraid?

The year is1964 and you are a young Black man driving down a dark road on your way to Meridian, Mississippi with two Jewish associates, when you see the bright lights of a car in your rearview mirror. Then, you see a flashing red light and know that it is a police vehicle.

Do you feel safe or are you forever regretful?

As a Black man in the year 2010, you're driving through Chicago's Englewood community and you quite appropriately stop at a stop sign.  Before you can pull off, four Black men pull up next to your car.

Are you scared?

Where do you as a Black American feel safe?

Where do you feel threatened?

Why are we still afraid?

Haven't we been afraid long enough?

_____

_____

_____

_____

_____

# 2

When you support Black causes and push Black agendas are you being prejudiced?   Or are you being pro-Black?

Are other ethnic-based organizations racist when they create race-based platforms to push their agenda?

_____

_____

_____

_____

*3*

What does it mean—to be poor—in America?

Is there anything wrong with living in the projects?

Is poverty an acceptable way of life?

At what point, will you no longer feel poor?

What is required for you and your family to feel secure financially?

? ? ? ? ?

I was absent from school the morning that the librarian allegedly told a class of sixth-graders that "they were too stupid to know that they were poor."

Upon my return to school that afternoon, the little news reporter in the making headed directly for me and hit me with that headline.

I could feel her bitterness as she angrily asked me, "Do you know what Mrs. _____ said to us this morning? Did you hear?"

My reaction might have been different from hers, as she felt even at her young age the stink and insult of classism. As she was going on and on about it, I keep hearing the word "poor" over and over again in my head. She informed everyone within listening range that she was not poor and that her mother worked every day.

Apparently, when the child went home for her lunch break, she shared the lessons learned in school that morning with her mother. It appeared that the child's mother didn't appreciate the topic presentation and told the child to tell the librarian that she would be up to the school the next morning to speak with her about the little revelation that she had shared with the students.

Also, according to the little conveyer of messages, the librarian additionally let them know that "they were too stupid to know that they lived in the ghetto."

What self-image did this person paint in the minds of those small children on that day? On that day, did that person feel lifted on an imaginary pedestal above those "poor, stupid, ghetto children"?

Even now, I laugh as I picture the librarian imagining herself in a "class" above those children. Did she really, really believe that the creators, perpetrators, and performers of these "self-proclaimed" class systems even envisioned her, as she obviously did, as a part of their class?

# *4*

**As** a young man, did you wear your hair processed in the 1940s, '50s or '60s?

How do you now feel about straightening your hair - and do you consider it an attempt to emulate the hair texture of the white male?

When you watch the videos of soul singers dancing across the stage in that era, with their lye-straighten haired and that side part, what crosses your mind?

When did you go "natural" or do you still process your hair?

---

---

# 5

Who do you give homage to both present and past for their contribution to the Black struggle?

---

---

---

---

---

# 6

Look in the mirror.

Who is looking back at you?  A Black man?  An African woman?

Define you.  What do you call yourself?  African, Black, Afro, Negro, Niger, Negar, Nigga, or

Colored — How do you wish to be addressed? Why?

How did the word "nigger" originate? Are you a nigger? How do you feel about the use of the word? Do you permit others to call you a nigger? Why?

Can you define yourself without saying that you are a Black man or Black woman? Or, is the ideology of Blackness interwoven and a defining aspect of your character? DNA? Personality? Being? Existence?

_____

_____

_____

_____

_____

# *7*

Can you remember when you began to "label" yourself as a Black, Negro, Colored, or African-American?

Who told you how you should be categorized in that manner and under what circumstances did they tell you?

How did this recognition of self come about and how did this knowledge affect you then? How does it affect you now?

How do you respond when asked "What is your ethnic group?" Why?

_____

_____

_____

_____

_____

# ? ? ? ? ?

Until I was 13 my family lived five lots down from the old Comiskey ballpark on 35th and Princeton in Chicago.

There sat the ballpark, all big and white and dominating. Across from the ballpark on 35th Street was "The Stand," which was said to have been owned by a young Italian guy named Tony. (It is rumored that he was sentenced to 20+ years for murder, or actually took a murder rap for one of the higher-ups.)

This same Tony also owned the large lot next to the hotdog stand that was used for parking. (Tony said that he did not steal my grandmother's home, (described below) but that the Irish asshole who owned the tavern on 35th Street stole it. But that's another story.)

Next, there was Miss Ann's cute little red house with the German Shepard dog named Ricky. Well, Miss Ann became a Mrs. when she married the widower who lived on the other side of us, in a gray brick two-story.

Then, there was us. Red. Mattie. The Perdues. The Youngs. In a tacky, brown-framed, two-flat, which in my earliest memories had no tub, but did have the most beautiful purple and white orchids that came up every spring and filled the entire front yard. We took baths in one of those old gray tin washtubs. Coal was used for the cooking stove in the kitchen and in the potbelly stove in the living room, which was used to keep that room—and only that room— warm in the winters. The refrigerator was actually an ice box. (Yes, I remember the ice man and the coal-delivery man.) But, those are very early memories and eventually there was a gas stove and a refrigerator … but still no bathtub.

Strangely enough, my grandfather lived directly across the street in a nice red-brick two-flat with porcelain bathtubs, oil heat, gas stove, nice refrigerator, and a new wife. (But, then, that too is another story.)

The train tracks to the west of the park divided the Bridgeport community and my community. If you crossed the line on either side of those tracks you would be reminded of the color of your skin.

It's difficult—no, it's almost impossible for most to pinpoint the place or the space in time when that first bite of prejudice sent that pang of pain through you and started something that would never be stopped, no matter how many "African-Americans" are elected as president of the USA.

Maybe you can, but I can't say when I actually became aware of the differences in skin color and the roles that you were expected to assume according to your hue. We could all have been affected by words or deeds carried out but long forgotten, except that the effects have become a part of our character and form how we view our world—how we see color.

My earliest memories regarding the differences in Black people and white people come back to me as I recall my grandmother rushing us children from in front of the house whenever there was a baseball game at the ballpark. We'd sit on the top stairs of the brown two-flat watching what seemed like a never ending parade of people pass our house from the south toward the ballpark.

As the number of marchers dwindled, we would periodically volunteer or be chosen to run down and do a sighting to see if any more were coming our way.

After all, this ballgame thing was taking up important play time. If we saw one or two of them still dragging along way down the street, we'd wait. I remember hollering up, "I see two more," or "four more." Or, "they're still coming."
"Or, here comes some more of them."

Eventually! Finally! We'd holler back and say that that was it. We were then free to play—free to pick up where we left off on our game again in front of our home.

I don't recall feeling prejudiced (probably didn't know what it was at that time), or hate, but I did know that it was just taking too long for *them* to get past our house. They looked strange to me, but this happened often enough that they no longer looked strange after a while. Some would smile and we'd smile back. Come to think of it, I've wondered what they thought as they passed Blacks on both sides of the street watching them as they passed by on their way to the ballpark.

When I reach way back in my memory, I do recall wondering why their clothes were so white and bright and clean. Now, don't get me wrong—before we played in the evening, we were fed and bathed, so it was not a feeling of inferiority. But, as a child I didn't realize, as I do now, that that's what you do in the summer time. You wear whites.

It just seemed like so much white.

## ? ? ? ? ?

The second, most vivid early memory of race/color differences came while watching my grandmother, Mattie Perdue, having to mentally and emotionally prepare herself to go to the A&P on 35th and Halsted in the "white folks' neighborhood." I recall her saying, "I hate to go over there. You have to be careful of those white people. But they've got a sale over there at that A&P and I want to go over there and get me some of that coffee."

Watching her, I wasn't quite sure what she was doing, but I saw something different about her as she started getting ready for that particular trip. Or, maybe, I was just moving on into an age group where you began to pay attention to certain things. Like any child, I was anxious to get to that store.

There was no discussion about the proper way to behave around white folks. She offered no check list or instructions.

She demonstrated.

We would ride the 35th Street bus to Halsted. And as we walked to the stores and through the stores, I watched her as she engaged her audience—as she stepped into this new role that she had chosen to play. She'd walk through the "white folks' neighborhood" humbling herself and smiling and nodding as though to say, "See me—I'm a harmless, good-natured Negro."

I remember watching her carry on with this performance and getting angry about it. I was angry at her and angry at the white folks. I understood what she was doing. Nothing felt right about it. Not the performance, not the risk, not for the coffee. And, at the same time that she was carrying out this performance, she seemed to be prancing through their neighborhood and laughing in their faces.

She seemed to be entertaining herself.

There was a smirk on her face behind the smile. It was as though she were dancing. I was astonished. My grandmother was almost 60 years old and it seemed that she wanted to giggle as she moved in and out through the crowds.

I do remember asking myself, What is she doing? Why doesn't she stop doing that?

Another reason that day remains a part of me is because during the bus ride back home, we sat facing each other and I've always had the impression that she was looking for a response, some sort of reaction from me. She was just sitting there staring at me, looking for something in me that would give her an indication of how I felt about the whole performance.

I was just a small child and I can't remember my exact thoughts, but I do remember thinking that she was checking to see if I was embarrassed by her performance. I did everything in my power to *not* show her that I was indeed ashamed, and even tried to casually start a conversation. And it worked—I witnessed a change in her and she seemed to put it behind her as we moved on toward home.

I never saw her do that again.

We didn't discuss it, but watching her maneuver through the white community sparked a lot of ideas in my mind about the relationship between Blacks and whites. But it did not instill in me the idea that I should become one of those "harmless, good-natured Negroes."

## *8*

In the presidential election of 2008, did you vote for Barack Hussein Obama?  Why?

_____

_____

_____

_____

_____

## *9*

How do you feel when you walk down the street with a white woman or man that you are intimately involved with and others give you "that look"?

What are your thoughts when you watch interracial couples in an intimate situation?

Would you choose a partner outside of your ethnic group?  If yes, which race would you **not** date or marry?  Why?

If you choose only to select a marriage partner from outside of your own race, what would be your reasons for that choice?

_____

_____

_____

_____

_____

# *10*

What educational or service programs are most needed in the Black community?

Name the one thing, that if it were immediately implemented within and throughout the Black community, would have a positively phenomenal impact on our people?

Is it doable?

If yes, why has it not been done?

*11*

Are you a republican or a democrat?  In what way has either of these political parties been of service to you?

Have you voted for the same elected officials for the past eight, 12, or 20 years?

Look around at your community. Should you vote for your currently elected officials, once again, in the next election?   Did they earn it, or are you simply trying to be ensure that they stay employed, while you remain unemployed?

# 12

Are there too many Black churches?

Do Black people need to get on their knees more or get off of their knees?

# *13*

With all of the allegations regarding the founder and the "true" intent of Planned Parenthood, what is your perspective on Planned Parenthood and birth control for women of color?

What is your position on Planned Parenthood, or similar organizations in Africa?

_____

_____

_____

_____

_____

# *14*

Do you celebrate Kwanzaa?

What family/cultural traditions do you celebrate?

---

---

---

---

# *15*

Fifty million dead. Fifty million dead. Reportedly, 37% of all abortions are performed on Black women. Our silence on the mass murder of approximately 15 million babies since 1973 is deafening.

Where is the outrage?

---

---

---

---

# *16*

**Why** did you move into an all-white neighborhood?  (But it's not all white any more, is it?)

Why do you live in an all-Black community?

_____

_____

_____

_____

# *17*

**Are** you Black enough?

Does it bother you when someone is "acting" white?

What criteria are we using as the yard stick to measure Blackness?

# *18*

**What** does freedom mean to you?   Free to do what?

Are you free?

What do you do with your freedom?

What would you do if that freedom was taken away from you today?

_____

_____

# *19*

# Corporations are now free to arbitrate racial discrimination complaints, although most arbitrators in the United States are white. Do you feel that a member of another ethnic group can make a fair decision in a case regarding racial discrimination?

_____

_____

_____

_____

_____

# *20*

# Has your child been or is your child now part of the foster care system?

Is your son or daughter doing jail time?

How did you let this happen to your child?

How did we let this happen to our children?

_____

_____

_____

_____

_____

# *21*

Do you suspect that most men and women who have  spent time in the prison system have engaged in homosexual activity?

Are boys who wear saggy pants displaying homosexual tendencies?

Homosexuality in the Black community — where does it fit?  Or, does it fit?

_____

_____

## 22

Has the Black American benefited from integration?

If yes, point out those benefits.

If no, what would have been a better solution?

Is America integrated?

Has busing improved the education of the Black child?

## *23*

Do you feel, in 2010, that Blacks are welcomed in corporate America or are we still like Sam Greenlee's character in "Spook Who Sat by the Door?

In the spirit of the memory of Ralph Ellison's "Invisible Man," are we "visible" Americans?

_____

_____

_____

_____

_____

## *24*

Can you trace your historical roots across the ocean before our time in this land?  If not, how does it make you feel to run into a wall when you try to reach beyond Mississippi, Georgia, or Alabama for your personal family history?

---------------

---------------

---------------

---------------

---------------

# *25*

**What** should be the direction of the education and training of the next generation of Black Americans?

What is the significance of the Black college?

What preparation today will be of the greatest benefit to our race tomorrow?  Do we need another opera singer, ballerina, golfer?

Are we still being "mis-educated?

---------------

---------------

---------------

---

---

# 26

Are we reading the incorrect/false/misleading accounts of our history?  What is the true history of the African in American?

Who are the designated keepers of our legacies?

---

---

---

---

# 27

Are you pierced and tattooed because you've seen Africans pierced or are you following a punk-rock sort of mindset?

What is the meaning (from a Black perspective) of the nose, tongue and eyebrow piercings?

Why are Black men wearing two diamond earrings? (Isn't that what white women do when they dress up and want to exhibit a certain status or class?)

Are we developing, creating and redefining Black culture?  Or, are we once again letting others define our culture for us?

_____

_____

_____

_____

_____

## *28*

Have you been a victim of child molestation? By whom?

Is there a cover up of molestation in the Black community?

Who is keeping the secrets and when are we
going to start pointing fingers at the molesters
so that they will not continue to molest children
in the same family and community?

_____

_____

_____

_____

_____

# 29

Brown, cocoa, sepia, yellow, red, tan?   How do
you describe yourself in the Black rainbow?

Is the skin-color rating system among Black people
real or imaginary?

If you believe that a skin-color rating system does
exist within the Black race, how do you rate yourself?
How do you rate others?

_____

_____

_____

_____

_____

# *30*

Are we living in the past when we speak of the enslavement of Africans? Should we forget it and just get on with our lives?

Have you watched news depictions of the civil rights movement? Lynching? Dogs? Hoses? Murders? Assassinations?

Should this all just be forgotten?

_____

_____

_____

_____

# 31

When you hire non-Blacks to act as your attorney, handle your gardening, construction, and maintenance; do your nails or work for you in other capacities—do you really have a right to complain about the plight of the young Black male when you wouldn't even hire him to cut your grass?

Do you have a right to complain about the direction of our race, (or lack of such) when you don't contribute to the well-being of our race?

Do the dollars of non-Blacks flow through your business? What percentage of your customers are non-Blacks?

What percentage of your income do you give away to other ethnic groups? And what have you received in return?

## 32

Are we putting our energy and resources in the right places?  For example, was Jena 6 worth the effort?

Was the Million Man March a success?  Why?  Why not?

_____

_____

_____

_____

_____

## 33

Can you attend an all-white event and not be distracted by the fact that everyone else is white?

Are you comfortable with whites in so-called Black venues (*i.e.,* Blues Festival, etc.)?

## 34

We have the largest number of Black millionaires in US history and the largest number of elected officials, but can you tell the difference?

Where are *our* mega-malls? *Our* skyscrapers? *Our* Macy's and Saks Fifth Avenues? *Our* multi-residential complexes, condos, timeshares, manufacturing companies, import-export vessels, franchises, positions on the stock exchanges, airlines, etc?

Where does the money from these millionaires flow?

Where is the money from the Black churches flowing?

_____

_____

_____

_____

_____

# *35*

Do you know anyone who has been beaten or shot by the police?

_____

_____

_____

_____

# 36

**Are** Black women louder than women of other races?

_____

_____

_____

_____

_____

# 37

**Was** Mayor Harold Washington murdered?

_____

_____

_____

_____

---

# 38

Do you really give a damn about OJ Simpson?
More importantly, does OJ give a damn about you?

_____

_____

_____

_____

_____

# 39

When we look at the history of the African in America, we know that not only have we been held down physically, but also emotionally and psychologically. During those periods, our creativity and genius took on other forms. We kept pushing forth. But, we know that, as a result, we have not blossomed and grown to our full extent in this country.

Here and now in 2010 — What is holding us down?

_____

_____

_____

_____

_____

# ? ? ? ? ?

I heard a voice and when I looked up from what I was doing, there was this very old white woman pulling out a chair and sitting across from me. She said something about a son or a daughter (in-law?) looking at a condo model and waved her hand as to dismiss them. (I was a loan officer working on the weekends on a condo-conversion project in Chicago's South Shore community. My job was to prequalify prospective buyers.)

Here we sat at the same small round table in the back room of this condo floor model. There she was talking to me as though she were determined to do as much of it as possible in the few minutes she had out that day. Her words were coming at me in a rush.

When I determined that she was not a loan prospect, I was disappointed and I was about to ignore her. But then I started listening to her story and I became aware of the fact that there was more to this meeting.

I became sad and angry because in those few moments with her, I was beginning to understand how so much can be taken from a person without them even knowing that it was theirs to lose.

She told me that she had been on TV and that she'd hosted her own talk show. She said that one day she just decided that she wanted to be on TV. She had never done this before but thought that it looked like a lot of fun. She decided that she would try it, so she walked into a TV studio, discussed her idea, and got her very own talk show.

She was a tickled by the fact that she was able to talk her way into getting a show without having any experience. She said that she was on TV for quite some time and that it had been a pretty big show.

Don't ask me who she was because I didn't recognize her. But, I do remember her saying that "I just decided that that was what I wanted to do and I did it."

I don't know remember anything else that this woman said to me. Not really. If there was another sound in the room, I didn't hear it—it was like I stepped into a fog.

I was sitting there just wondering about how it felt to live a life without doubt clouding your choices? Without colored-only signs? Or, without your mind being turned against your own skin color? Living without being ashamed of your own brownness or trying to turn it into a lighter shade?

In my mother's or my grandmother's time, you didn't just get up one day and say that you wanted a TV show. You didn't even just get up one morning and even believe that you could have your TV show. You certainly didn't just get up one day and walk into a TV studio (not through the front door!), and tell them your idea for a television show.

And, here sat this old white woman, maybe about 70 years old, all chit-chatty about the whole thing.

Because she had lived her life without the colored-only signs before her eyes and forever a part of her memory.

Because she had lived a life where her dreams were not stomped down by ugly, hurting words, spat upon, blistered with whips, washed away by water hoses, attacked by dogs, murdered by assassins.

No one told her that she could not dream.

She could sat there in that small room with me, a Black woman who was two generations away from her, and reminisce about this accomplishment in her life.

Our paths were crossing at this tiny table, in this small, cluttered room and she didn't know a thing about being Black.

And I still don't know anything about being white.

**? ? ? ? ?**

# *40*

Do you feel that "Black" celebrities with their blond hair and light contacts are qualified to stand and represent Black womanhood to our future Black women?

What about Black male sports figures, entertainers, politicians and college professors who date and marry white women?

What messages are they sending to our young people?

Are they still considered Black?

_____

_____

_____

_____

_____

# 41

Do you as a Black person think that you are better than people of other ethnic groups?

Do you feel insecure and inferior around non-Blacks?

Do you feel that you must constantly prove your "worthiness" when you are in the company and employ of other ethnics groups?

_____

_____

_____

_____

_____

# 42

You've just received a letter offering you a very generous monetary gift and the only requirement is that you must relocate.

Where would you consider moving and why?

Where is there a better place for you?

_____

_____

_____

_____

_____

# *43*

## What is the current state of relationships between the Black man and the Black woman?

_____

_____

_____

_____

_____

## *44*

**Are** Blacks depicted accurately in the media?

What sources do you feel best tell the story of Black life in America -- on a daily basis?

What American publication(s) best represent the Black American experience?

Can a publication owned and editorialized by non-Blacks provide "truth" in publication to Black Americans?

---

---

---

---

# *45*

Are you concerned when you view the scenes of poverty, disease, famine, violence and war in Africa and other parts of the world, or does Black America have its own problems?

_____

_____

_____

_____

_____

# *46*

Define marriage.

Define the role of a husband.

Define the role of a wife.

Have you ever had a discussion with your child about choosing a mate?

What are we teaching the next generation about these roles and how these roles fit into the survival of our people?

Give an example of the wedding, marriage, vows or process that is representative of Black Americans?

_____

_____

_____

_____

_____

# 47

What are your true feelings about people of other ethnic groups?  How do you really feel about white people?

_____

_____

_____

_____

_____

# *48*

In the scope of the one-drop theory, does one drop of African blood make you an African?

If you can now be classified as 56% white (according to your DNA results), will you refer to yourself as Caucasian, marry a white person, and then holler racism when you are stopped by the cops for driving while Black?

_____

_____

_____

_____

_____

# *49*

Do you really want to live your life pretending that color doesn't matter?

_____

_____

_____

_____

_____

# *50*

When you are out and about and a Black person starts talking loud, are you embarrassed?

_____

_____

_____

# *51*

Do we as Black people have an American agenda? Is there a place for us on the American landscape?

Where are we, as a people, on the international landscape? Do we even have a voice or a place?

# *52*

The failures of the Black child in the educational system are the responsibility/fault of whom?  The educators?  The parents?

If we take credit for the successes, why should we not take responsibility for the failures?

# *53*

**Why** do some Black Muslims straighten their hair and wear business suits?

What do you think about Africans straightening their hair and wearing business suits?

_____

_____

_____

_____

_____

# *54*

**What** is Black beauty?   What is Black style?
What is Black culture?

_____

_____

_____

_____

_____

# *55*

**What** cause, person or principle would you give your life for?

Are you willing to give your life for the current American military agendas?

_____

_____

_____

_____

_____

# *56*

Who is controlling the minds of our boys and girls?

Have the children of today become who they are because of the lack of direction from adults?

Or because of the direction that adults are leading them?

_____

_____

_____

_____

_____

# *57*

What have you given? (You, not your ancestors.)
What will you give?

What are you asking of America?

---------------------------------------

---------------------------------------

---------------------------------------

---------------------------------------

---------------------------------------

## *58*

**Has** Section 8, Affirmative Action, and welfare programs served as our reparations?  Should affirmative-action programs be eliminated?

---------------------------------------

---------------------------------------

---------------------------------------

---------------------------------------

---------------------------------------

## 59

The son that you raised is beating your daughter-in-law.   What are you going to do about it?

You husband is beating you, now what are you going to do about that?

_____

_____

_____

_____

## 60

Has the publication of some magazines by Black Americans, from early times to now, done more harm than good to the community by their imitation and allegiance to white society?

_____

_____

_____

_____

_____

# *61*

How can we as a Black people collectively define and formulate solutions to our own problems?

_____

_____

_____

_____

_____

# 62

As the ranks of Blacks in non-Black colleges and universities began to swell, did those generations of Blacks, miss the opportunity to move our race toward a collective agenda by the creation of sororities and frats which may have fed into an ideal of elitist and separation that may not have been the most beneficial mindset for us, as a people, at that particular time?

At that very vulnerable time in African American history, did our brightest minds ("educated or mis-educated") miss the chance to create a great and different world structure for our people?

Is it possible that those generations missed the opportunity to lead our people in, up and through a powerful Black movement?

# *63*

Who are the protectors of our young girls?

As men in their 20s, 30s, and 40s and beyond, look lustfully down the bosoms and at the bodies of our young girls …?

As they engage in sexual activity with these young women openly and without penalty …?

As men of age with the mentality of boys holler at our young girls and disrespect them as they walk about our communities …?

What are we going to do about it?

Are we the protectors of our young girls?

---------------------------------------------------

---------------------------------------------------

---------------------------------------------------

---------------------------------------------------

# *64*

**Who** are your heroes?   Who do you most admire?

_____

_____

_____

_____

_____

## ? ? ? ? ?

I was very young.  12 years old.  Kenneth Johnson was younger. He was 5 years old.  We lived on the first floor of a small two-flat and Kenneth and his family lived upstairs.  The Johnsons were in their late 20s and had four children; whenever the young couple wanted to go out, I was the children's playmate/babysitter.

It would be a grand time — every time.  We'd play games, play school, but most importantly there was no screaming, and beatings, or arguing.  Although I was young, they knew that they were safe with me because I loved being in charge and I just loved small children.

The elderly couple who had previously lived in that apartment had been the owners of the building. They had four foster children and Kenneth's mother was their granddaughter. When the mother died, all of the children, except Robert, were returned to their parents or to the state. Maybe there was no place for him to go. He moved in with the elderly gentleman and his new wife in their home, two doors down.

Robert and I had been at war since I was small enough to crawl under a bed. That's my earliest memory of him chasing me and grabbing me in a sexual manner. I would come to play with the other kids and he'd begin grabbing me and touching me and I would run and slide under his mother's bed. He was trying to get me from under there, but he was too big to crawl under there and reach me. I knew even then that he was afraid of getting caught, so he coached me out with smoothing words that he was not going to bother me.

This game (attack) of cat and mouse went on and on. I was just as intense and determined and he could not get a grip on me. I had always sent the signal that I was ready for a fight. The first few times, I could crawl under the bed, but after a while I was too big and I had to stand and fight or take flight.

As Robert got older and bigger and stronger, he became more aggressive. It became harder and harder to fight him off, but he came knowing that there would be a battle. I don't believe that he was yet old enough to be that sure of himself.

Fast forward to my being 12 and Robert being 17 years of age. Somehow he had gotten wind of the fact that I was upstairs with the children.

We were sitting on the sofa watching TV when the door opened. All of us turned and looked; as he spoke, he moved from the door over to me. "I'm going to get you today. I'm going to get me some today."

I was thinking, How did he know that I was up here?

Fear rose up in me and as I prepared myself for a fight. I felt fear. When he moved in for the attack, I was still sitting on the sofa because it all seemed like one motion from the door to me. There was no time for anything else.

As we struggled, he was on my right side sitting on the sofa and trying to push me down into a lying position. He was trying to get a grip on my hands and arms and could not because I was swinging them all of the time. If he could have stopped me from hitting him, he could have mounted me. I kept fighting to keep control or to keep him from gaining control.

For some reason, I didn't want to start screaming because I didn't want to scare the children. Too late. I looked to my left and the three smaller children were huddled against the wall watching us. They had a bewildered, wild-eyed, and confused look on their faces (one of those "deer-caught-in-the-headlights" expressions).

Kenneth was standing in front of Robert, a little off to his right about a foot or two away from him. I can't say what he was thinking, but in retrospect, he was gauging the situation. Maybe at first, he didn't perceive that I was in danger. There was no fear in his face and I don't recall seeing any sense of panic in his eyes. This little boy was just standing there watching us do battle.

Then, things changed. It seemed fast and in slow-motion at the same time. Now I was the observer. I will never be sure, but maybe this little boy sensed, after giving the situation some thought, that I just might lose that battle. Quite unexpectedly.

Quite, quite wondrously, this 5-year-old boy leaped on this 17-year-old and began to beat him so viciously that he couldn't maintain his grip on me for having to defend himself against this child's blows.

Kenneth was beating him and screaming and screaming and screaming. "Take your hands off of her. You stop it. You stop it. You leave her alone." It was happening so fast. He was moving so fast that I could not keep up with what was happening. Those little arms were moving and swinging and clawing. It was like something flashing before my eyes. Watching it would make you say, "What the hell?"

Robert was not trying to hurt or injure him, but just trying to stop Kenneth from hitting him. Robert was laughing at him, at first. He thought that it was funny. He tried to grab his arms. Tried to calm him down. Tried to hang on to me. It didn't work out like he expected. He had to let go of me.

I was looking directly into Robert's face when that child wiped that smile off of his mug. He was taking a good look at that child attacking him. I watched the change taking place. I heard the change in his tone, his words, his whole being as he tried to assure Kenneth that he would not touch me again. He was trying to hold Kenneth down and tell him that he was going to stop and that he was not going to touch me. "Calm down man. Calm down." He kept saying, "OK man. OK man." He repeated these words to him over and over again.

I was frozen. I didn't know how to move. I only knew how to watch as a participant in a movie with a surprise ending that was never even written into the script.

Robert was finally able to calm Kenneth down and we both sat there staring at this little boy, who was sobbing and taking these huge loud breaths. The attack itself was a shock, but the hollering and crying took it over the edge. It seemed that that child had gotten so wound up that he couldn't come down immediately. He finally calmed and he told him one more time, "You leave her alone! Don't you bother her again!"

I was taken aback, as I sat there that day, but Robert was taken further. Robert told him that he would not touch me again. And he never did.

Without regard to the size or might of the enemy, this little boy moved into position, executed an attack, and was victorious. He left the enemy/potential rapist empty and impotent.

Robert stood up from the sofa as we all watched him straighten his clothes. He told me that he was sorry and that he would never, ever touch me again. He told me that I had nothing to worry about. I can only think that if shame had a smell, it would smell just like Robert Johnson.

Here and now, I wonder if Robert remembers the day that a 5-year-old boy became more man then he would ever be.

**? ? ? ? ?**

# *65*

What's was your most recent experience involving racial/color discrimination?   How did you handle/respond to the incident?

_____

_____

_____

_____

_____

# *66*

You know who's selling guns and drugs to our young people.

You know which adults are using the young people of this nation for their personal gratification.

Is it you? If it is not you, then what are you going to do about it?

_____

_____

_____

_____

_____

## *67*

# Define what ethics mean to you?

What is the moral creed or code within your family?

How do you pass forward your beliefs, family history, and traditions to your children?

What is the collective moral creed/code/agreement within the African-American community?

Should there be or can there be a collective moral code/creed/agreement among Black Americans?

_____

_____

_____

---

---

# 68

You have four children by three different men or women.  Is this to now be considered the norm?

Then, should those with a husband or wife and four children by the same partners be considered abnormal?

---

---

---

---

# 69

From age 18 to 40, in what could be considered your most financially formative years, every paycheck you earn shows a huge deduction for child support from two or three different babies' mamas. How do you feel about that?

What can we do to stop this from happening to the next generation?

_____

_____

_____

_____

# 70

What constitutes the mental, emotional and physical states of Black America?

Are we making the worst "lifestyle" choices for ourselves and our families?

What would it take to collectively move us down a path of "better" life choices?

_____

_____

_____

_____

_____

# 71

You've just had unprotected sex.

Then you will once again have unprotected sex with someone else.   Should you be considered a dangerous weapon?   Should you be considered a threat to our community?  Should we look upon you as an enemy to our people?

Should we categorize that person who permits you to lie with them and engage in unprotected sex, as suicidal or mentally ill?

Maybe before mounting your next victim or before being mounted, we should ask if it would be OK with them to share a lifetime 'bout of herpes or HIV/AID, or any other variety of very nasty things that can be spread between you and your sexual partners.

Or, how about simply asking each other, the moment right before that "big moment"... "Hey! Would you like to make a baby that neither one of us really wants?"

Or, how about this... "Let's have unprotected sex tonight, and although we will never, ever have sex again, how about you pay me child support for the next, let's say, eighteen years? Deal?"

Or, that instead of giving your spouse or girlfriend your love and affection, how about you give them a STD?

# *72*

What do you consider to be your native language?

Is there any such a thing as Black English?

If Black Americans, along with our African brothers and sisters, were to choose a language to unite all of us as a people, linguistically, what language would be the best choice as an international language for our people?

How can we proceed to make such a transition a reality?

# *73*

How many Africans do you know, personally?

_____

_____

_____

_____

# *74*

Define Black music.   Black food.   Black dancing.

_____

_____

_____

## 75

**What** is the oldest Black business in America?

## 76

**Do** you blame the Africans for our enslavement?

Do you blame our Black ancestors for us being held captive for such a long period of time?

---

---

---

---

---

# *77*

# What would you define as the good life for Black Americans?

---

---

---

---

---

# *78*

What is the major source of income for you and your family?   Employment?   Self-employment?

Are you satisfied with your current income level?

Are you satisfied with your current level of skills, education or trade?

What are your plans for additional training or education?

_____

_____

_____

_____

# *79*

Do you find yourself acting/performing one way for "white" folks and another way when you are in the company of "Black" folks?   Why?

_____

_____

_____

_____

_____

# *80*

Are you old enough to remember your parents or grandparents telling you where you could or should not eat, walk or sit, because in some causes your "inappropriate" actions could cause you to lose your life, given the real and continuous threat to our people from white people?

Do you remember being told not to look white people in their eyes, to hold your head down and humble yourself when you spoke to them or to watch what you said in their presence?

Did you ever have to use the back door?

What are your true feelings about these experiences?

_____

_____

_____

_____

_____

# *81*

Have any of these questions made you feel uncomfortable?

Which ones?  In what way?  Why?

_____

_____

_____

_____

# *82*

Has it been possible for you to complete this process without recognizing the need for change within yourself, your home, your community or your world view?

What will you do about it?

## *83*

# Shall we overcome someday?

_____

_____

_____

_____

_____

# In Closing

Thank each of you for being part of this experience.

There are no absolute responses to these questions, and this experience will probably generate more questions than answers, simply because we as a people -- like the universe -- are forever evolving.

We do hope that this open dialogue will prompt changes, whether small or large, whether individually or collectively, throughout the Black community.

If we do nothing, nothing will change and we'll be having this same conversation in 2011.

Are you willing to pick up the 2011 edition of "Asking Ourselves The Tough Questions – The 2011 Experience" and face the truth, the sad truth that *nothing* has changed?

Register at *www.AskingOurselvesTheToughQuestions.com* to share your views and stories on the questions presented in our first edition of this series.

We hope that you've enjoyed the journey and even more so, we hope that you've learned more about yourself for having made a decision to be a part of the process.

## *WHERE WERE HER WOMEN?*

**By Sonja Cassandra Perdue**

For Tina
April 11, 2001

I was there.
I'll be the first to admit it.
She was years ahead of me.
And from our beginning, I was running right behind her.
I caught up with her and passed her.
Not because I was smarter or quicker,
but, because she was standing still.

> I kept moving.
> Not even looking back.

Today, I turned and watched her,
There were others with her.   But, she was standing alone.

> None said, "Don't bend."
> So she bent.

> No one said, "Don't marry trash, even if you're feeling a bit trashy."
> So she bedded them.   Married them.   Had their babies.

Life's darkest moments left permanent tears behind her eyes.
Thirty odd years folded up around her leaving scar-after-scar embedded in her
spirit.

Where were her examples of the sharpness, the pride, the loving, the strength, the
creativity, the tenacity, the strut, the struggle, and the blackness in Black women?

She was listening.
She was waiting.
But, she never heard the words "and still we rise."
So, that is where she lies.
She is looking up.   But, from where she is, she can't see the sky.

WHERE WERE HER WOMEN?

**"Asking Ourselves The Tough Questions"** is a formalized, five part "Q & A" session that began in July 2010 and ends with the last publication in 2014.

This series of books will challenge Black America to collectively engage in a dialogue that will initiate solutions to our collective concerns and issues.  Armed with the knowledge that we are without limitations in spirit or mind, we march forward, together to fulfill the hopes and dreams of our people.

My vision for the 2014 publication:  "Black American:  Our Questions - Answered."

Watch for our radio and television broadcasts, where we travel across this country and ask Black America "The Tough Questions."

# BLACK AMERICA

## ASKING OURSELVES
## THE TOUGH QUESTIONS

## BOOK TWO

## The 2011 Experience

## By Sonja Cassandra Perdue

One hundred people will be selected by the author to participate in *Asking Ourselves The Tough Questions – The 2011 Experience*.

Those chosen will have their response to select questions from the 2010 edition published in our 2011 edition.

Along with their answers, to a question from the 2010 edition, those selected will be given the dynamic opportunity of asking our readers the tough question of their choosing to be included in *Asking Ourselves The Tough Questions – The 2011 Experience*.

If you wish to join us, please see the registration agreement posted on our website.  www.AskingOurselvesTheToughQuestions.com.

# BOOK ORDER FORM

To order your copy of "**Black American:  Asking Ourselves The Tough Questions - Book One 2010.**"

Complete the following order form and send with check or money order made payable to:

Sonja Perdue
28 E. Jackson, P597
Chicago, IL 60604

To place an order online visit:

**www.AskingOurselvesTheToughQuestions.com**

<u>**BOOK ORDER FORM**</u>

# Black American:  Asking Ourselves The Tough Questions - Book One 2010

**Please Print Clearly**

First Name: _____ Last Name: _____

Title:  _____

Organization Name:_____

Mailing Address: _____

_____

City / State / Zip: _____

Telephone:_____ Fax: _____

E-mail:  _____

Number of Copies Requested (shipping and handling included):

_____ Within the U.S. / $20.00 per book (media mail)

_____ Outside of the U.S. / $24.00 per book (surface shipping: 1 month delivery)

If you are interested in placing an order for  more than 10 copies please call for rate at (312) 239-8835

*Personal or bank checks should be made payable to: Sonja Perdue*

*Total Enclosed $_____*

**Thank you for your order.**

## A Waking Death

Forgive me.

    For my body, spirit and consciousness has been asleep.

    But now my mind has wings and I am are ready to fly.


**Black America**

**Sonja Cassandra Perdue 2010**

?

?

?

?

?

2010

www.ingramcontent.com/pod-product-compliance
Lightning Source LLC
Chambersburg PA
CBHW062049280526
45788CB00003B/1158